Presented to

Mr. Richard Martin
1300 Greencroft Dr., Apt. 71
Goshen IN 46526-5193

_____

By

_____

On the Occasion of

_____

Date

_____

IN HIS WORDS

What Did Jesus Say?

Compiled by
Ellen W. Caughey

BARBOUR
PUBLISHING, INC.
Uhrichsville, Ohio

Published by Barbour Publishing, Inc., P.O. Box 719, Uhrichsville, OH 44683 http:\\www.barbourbooks.com

Member of the
Evangelical Christian
Publishers Association

Printed in the United States of America.

Contents

Preface

Preface

For as the rain cometh down, and the snow from heaven, and returneth not thither, but watereth the earth, and maketh it bring forth the bud, that it may give seed to the sower, and bread to the eater: so shall my word be that goeth forth out of my mouth: it shall not return unto me void, but it shall accomplish that which I please, and it shall prosper in the thing whereto I sent it.

ISAIAH 55: 10, 11

Jesus' words are meant to be planted. Sent by the Father to earth on a mission like no other, Jesus the Son was given a message to share with the world, a message that would endure until the Son's return.

Jesus' words—words that cut to the chase, or to the heart of any issue—are the essence of what it means to be a Chris-tian. What does it mean to be saved? How can I learn to forgive? Is it possible to find lasting peace, to be truly happy? How can I know God's plan for me? Through parables and plain words, Jesus answers these critical questions of life, and much, much more.

How's your garden growing these days? Are new and glorious blossoms of insight filling your days, are you forming deeper roots of under-standing of God's Word so that when crises arise, your garden won't shrivel up? Or are you walking through a stony field, tripping over warring vines, accosted by thorns and pesky insects?

In His Words is a packet of healthy, life-giving seeds. Ready to be planted, ready to grow, guaranteed to thrive—forever.

PART I:

His Mission

WHO IS JESUS?

First and foremost, He is God's Son,
but Jesus is also the
Advocate of every believer.

Verily, verily, I say unto you, before Abraham
was, I am. JOHN 8:58

Jesus was born in human form
on earth but He has always existed,
from before the beginning of time.

All power is given unto me in heaven and in
earth. MATTHEW 28:18

. . .If God were your Father, ye would love me:
for I proceeded forth and came from God; neither
came I of myself, but he sent me. JOHN 8:42

Jesus is God's Son,
sent to earth by His Father.

Not that any man
hath seen the Father,
save he which is of God,
he hath seen the Father.

JOHN 6:46

For the Son of man is Lord even of the sabbath day. MATTHEW 12:8

No laws are greater than Jesus,
even those that prohibited
work on the Sabbath.
He is Lord of every day!

———◆———

A prophet is not without honour, save in his own country, and in his own house.   MATTHEW 13:57

Jesus is a prophet like the prophets
of the Old Testament. . .
He too experienced ridicule
and rejection in
His "hometown" of Nazareth.

———◆———

The Son can do nothing of himself, but what he seeth the Father do: for what things soever he doeth, these also doeth the Son likewise.
JOHN 5:19

Jesus and God the Father
act as one.

How say they that Christ is David's son? And David himself saith in the book of Psalms, The Lord said unto my Lord, Sit thou on my right hand, till I make thine enemies thy footstool. David therefore called him Lord, how is he then his son?   LUKE 20:41-44

. . .I am not come of myself, but he that sent me is true, whom ye know not. But I know him: for I am from him, and he hath sent me.   JOHN 7:28, 29

For whether is greater, he that sitteth at meat, or he that serveth? is not he that sitteth at meat? but I am among you as he that serveth.

LUKE 22:27

Jesus is a servant,
humble and self-sacrificing.

For the Father loveth the Son, and sheweth him all things that himself doeth: and he will shew him greater works than these, that ye may marvel.

JOHN 5:20

All things are delivered unto me of my Father: and no man knoweth the Son, but the Father; neither knoweth any man the Father, save the Son, and he to whomsoever the Son will reveal him.

MATTHEW 11:27

*Jesus is the believer's
only link to
God the Father.*

———◆◇◆———

Verily, verily, I say unto you, I am the door of the sheep. All that ever came before me are thieves and robbers: but the sheep did not hear them. I am the door: by me if any man enter in, he shall be saved, and shall go in and out, and find pasture. The thief cometh not, but for to steal, and to kill, and to destroy: I am come that they might have life, and that they might have it more abundantly.

JOHN 10:7-10

*Jesus is
the only way
to heaven.*

I am the bread of life: he that cometh to me shall never hunger; and he that believeth on me shall never thirst. JOHN 6:35

. . .Thou hast given him [Jesus] power over all flesh, that he should give eternal life to as many as thou hast given him. JOHN 17:2

*Jesus has the power to grant
eternal life to those who believe in Him.*

This is an evil generation: they seek a sign; and there shall no sign be given it, but the sign of Jonas the prophet. For as Jonas was a sign unto the Ninevites, so shall also the Son of man be to this generation. LUKE 11:29, 30

*Jesus is referring to Jonah, the minor prophet of
the Old Testament. After three days in the
stomach of a great fish, Jonah went to the
wicked city of Nineveh and urged the people to
repent. Likewise, Jesus, after three days in the
tomb, was raised from the dead as a sign
for the world to repent of sin.*

I am the way,
the truth, and the life:
no man cometh unto the Father,
but by me.

JOHN 14:6

———◆———

I am the good shepherd: the good shepherd giveth his life for his sheep.   JOHN 10:11

Thou sayest that I am a king. To this end was I born, and for this cause came I into the world, that I should bear witness unto the truth. Everyone that is of the truth heareth my voice.

     JOHN 18:37

Jesus is a king,
the King of Kings!
His kingdom, though,
is not confined
by time or space.

I am the true vine, and my Father is the husbandman. Every branch in me that beareth not fruit he taketh away: and every branch that beareth fruit, he purgeth it, that it may bring forth more fruit.

     JOHN 15:1, 2

Jesus is the embodiment
of a godly, fulfilling life.

I am come to send fire on the earth; and what will I, if it be already kindled?   Luke 12:49

> *Jesus inflames men and women*
> *with His testimony,*
> *but He also will judge—*
> *"send fire on" those*
> *who reject Him.*

———◆———

I tell you that, if these should hold their peace, the stones would immediately cry out.   LUKE 19:40

> *Jesus is referring to*
> *the multitude of disciples*
> *who greeted Him upon*
> *His triumphant entry into Jerusalem*
> *on what we call Palm Sunday.*
> *The Pharisees objected to*
> *the disciples' adoration of Jesus,*
> *but Jesus knew what was taking place*
> *was a fulfillment of Scripture.*
> *Jesus' reference to stones was not made in jest:*
> *He holds sway over*
> *all forms of nature!*

I am the good shepherd, and know my sheep, and am known of mine. As the Father knoweth me, even so know I the Father: and I lay down my life for the sheep. . .there shall be one fold, and one shepherd.   JOHN 10:14-16

Jesus is the ultimate sacrifice.
His death on the cross—
and His Resurrection—
has ensured that all who believe
will find eternal security
with Him in heaven.

WHY DID JESUS COME TO EARTH?

*Jesus came to earth so
that as many believe in Him
can truly be saved. . .yes, saved,
forgiven of and freed from
the downward spiral of sin,
assured of eternal life!*

This is the work of God, that ye believe on him whom he hath sent. JOHN 6:29

For God sent not his Son into the world to condemn the world; but that the world through him might be saved. JOHN 3:17

For the Son of man is come to seek and to save that which was lost. LUKE 19:10

I am come a light
into the world,
that whosoever
believeth on me
should not abide
in darkness.

JOHN 12:46

Repent: for the kingdom of heaven is at hand.

MATTHEW 4:17

They that be whole need not a physician, but they that are sick. . .for I am not come to call the righteous, but sinners to repentance.

MATTHEW 9:12, 13

The Son of man goeth as it is written of him. . .

MATTHEW 26:24

Jesus came to
fulfill prophecy.
His ministry on earth
had been foretold in almost
every book of the Old Testament.

———◆———

I was sent only to the lost sheep of Israel.

MATTHEW 15:24

Jesus came first
to bring the Gospel
to the Jews.

How is it that ye sought me? wist ye not that I must be about my Father's business? LUKE 2:49

*Jesus' earthly parents
had been searching for
the "lost" twelve year old in Jerusalem,
only to discover Him in the temple,
indeed going about
His Father's business,
imparting true understanding
of the Scriptures.*

The Spirit of the Lord is upon me, because he hath anointed me to preach the gospel to the poor; he hath sent me to heal the broken-hearted, to preach deliverance to the captives, and recovering of sight to the blind, to set at liberty them that are bruised. To preach the acceptable year of the Lord. LUKE 4:18, 19

*Jesus is not referring to a calendar "year"
but the period of time when
salvation would be proclaimed,
after the advent of His earthly birth
and until His Second Coming.*

The Son of man
must suffer many things,
and be rejected of
the elders and chief priests and scribes,
and be slain,
and be raised the third day.

LUKE 9:22

———◆———

Let us go into the next towns, that I may preach there also: for therefore came I forth.

MARK 1:38

*Jesus came to share in the most
personal way the news of salvation.*

I have many things to say and to judge of you: but he that sent me is true; and I speak to the world those things which I have heard of him.

JOHN 8:26

*Jesus came to affirm
the truth of God's Word.*

Thus it is written, and thus it behoved Christ to suffer, and to rise from the dead the third day: and that repentance and remission of sins should be preached in his name among all nations, beginning at Jerusalem.

LUKE 24:46, 47

*Jesus came to die as a once
and final payment for sin.*

If I then, your Lord and Master, have washed your feet: ye also ought to wash one another's feet. For I have given you an example, that ye should do as I have done to you.   JOHN 13:14, 15

Jesus came to earth to present Himself
as an example in all things,
even laboring at supposedly menial tasks.

———✦———

And whosoever will be chief among you, let him be your servant: even as the Son of man came not to be ministered unto, but to minister, and to give his life a ransom for many.   MATTHEW 20:27, 28

A ransom—
originally the price paid
to redeem a slave—
is what Jesus paid for us
by His death on the cross.

———✦———

The Son of man shall be betrayed into the hands of men: and they shall kill him, and the third day he shall be raised again.   MATTHEW 17:22, 23

I must work the works
of him that sent me,
while it is day:
the night cometh,
when no man can work.
As long as I am in the world,
I am the light of the world.

JOHN 9:4, 5

———⋅❈⋅———

Therefore doth my Father love me, because I lay down my life, that I might take it again. No man taketh it from me, but I lay it down of myself. I have power to lay it down, and I have power to take it again. This commandment have I received of my Father. JOHN 10:17, 18

Think not that I am come to send peace on earth: I came not to send peace, but a sword.

MATTHEW 10:34

Jesus knew that between those who
believe and those who refuse
to accept Him as God's Son,
there would always be discord.

———◆———

Now is my soul troubled; and what shall I say? Father, save me from this hour: but for this cause came I unto this hour. Father, glorify thy name.

JOHN 12:27, 28

As the time neared for Jesus' crucifixion,
Jesus agonized over His fate—
yet He knew that His ultimate sacrifice
must take place.

Ye sent unto John, and he bare witness unto the truth. But I receive not testimony from man: but these things I say, that ye might be saved.

JOHN 5:33, 34

*Jesus was referring to
the ministry of John the Baptist,
which preceded His own.
Jesus' testimony came
directly from
God the Father,
testimony that has the power
to save men and women
from the consequences
of their sins.*

For I came down from heaven, not to do mine own will, but the will of him that sent me. And this is the Father's will which hath sent me, that of all which he hath given me I should lose nothing, but should raise it up again at the last day.

JOHN 6:38, 39

*All who believe in Jesus,
who ask Him to be their Savior,
are promised eternal life.*

My meat is to do the will of him that sent me, and to finish his work.   JOHN 4:34

Verily, verily, I say unto you, Moses gave you not that bread from heaven; but my Father giveth you the true bread from heaven. For the bread of God is he which cometh down from heaven, and giveth life unto the world.   JOHN 6:32, 33

> *The bread given Moses—*
> *manna in the Sinai wilderness—*
> *lasted only one day.*
> *Jesus' "bread"—*
> *His Word—*
> *is life-giving and eternal.*

DID HE FULFILL HIS MISSION?

What God the Father directed
His Son to do was done...
but Jesus' mission continues
in subtle and explosive ways,
until He comes again.

When ye have lifted up the Son of man, then shall ye know that I am he, and that I do nothing of myself; but as my Father hath taught me, I speak these things. And he that sent me is with me; the Father hath not left me alone; for I do always those things that please him.   JOHN 8:28, 29

For the Father himself loveth you, because ye have loved me, and have believed that I came out from God. I came forth from the Father, and am come into the world: again, I leave the world, and go to the Father.   JOHN 16:27, 28

O righteous Father,
the world hath not known thee:
but I have known thee,
and these have known that
thou hast sent me.
And I have declared
unto them thy name,
and will declare it:
that the love wherewith thou hast
loved me may be in them,
and I in them.

JOHN 17:25, 26

————◆————

I have glorified thee on the earth: I have finished the work which thou gavest me to do. And now, O Father, glorify thou me with thine own self with the glory which I had with thee before the world was.   JOHN 17:4, 5

And now I come to thee; and these things I speak in the world, that they [believers in Jesus] might have my joy fulfilled in themselves.
                                                    JOHN 17:13

PART II:

His Message

IS THIS ALL
THERE IS TO LIFE?

Eternal life. . .
living with Jesus forever. . .
is yours if you believe that He is God's Son.

For God so loved the world, that he gave his only begotten Son, that whosoever believeth in him should not perish, but have everlasting life.

JOHN 3:16

And as Moses lifted up the serpent in the wilderness, even so must the Son of man be lifted up: that whosoever believeth in him should not perish, but have eternal life.   JOHN 3:14, 15

Jesus must suffer the torment
of crucifixion and then
be resurrected from death
back to life for those who believe
to gain eternal life.

Not every one that saith unto me, Lord, Lord, shall enter into the kingdom of heaven; but he that doeth the will of my Father which is in heaven.   MATTHEW 7:21

My kingdom is not of this world: if my kingdom were of this world, then would my servants fight, that I should not be delivered to the Jews: but now is my kingdom not from hence.   JOHN 18:36

And every one that hath forsaken houses, or brethren, or sisters, or father, or mother, or wife, or children, or lands, for my name's sake, shall receive an hundredfold, and shall inherit eternal life.   MATTHEW 19:29

*To those who sacrificed much
to spread the Gospel on earth
an additional reward in heaven will be given.
Jesus does not mean Christians
should leave their families
to serve Him.*

. . .If a man keep
my saying,
he shall never
see death.

JOHN 8:51

If thou canst believe, all things are possible to him that believeth. MARK 9:23

He that believeth and is baptized shall be saved; but he that believeth not shall be damned.

MARK 16:16

. .The kingdom of heaven is like unto treasure hid in a field; the which when a man hath found, he hideth, and for joy thereof goeth and selleth all that he hath, and buyeth that field.

MATTHEW 13:44

. . .The kingdom of heaven is like unto a merchant man, seeking goodly pearls: Who, when he had found one pearl of great price, went and sold all that he had, and bought it.   MATTHEW 13:45, 46

. . .The kingdom of heaven is like unto a net, that was cast into the sea, and gathered of every kind: Which, when it was full, they drew to shore, and sat down, and gathered the good into vessels, but cast the bad away.   MATTHEW 13:47, 48

. . .Except ye repent, ye shall all likewise perish.
LUKE 13:3

Did ye never read in the scriptures, The stone which the builders rejected, the same is become the head of the corner: this is the Lord's doing, and it is marvellous in our eyes?   MATTHEW 21:42

While the nation of Israel rejected Jesus—
the "stone"—as the Messiah,
Jesus became the foundation
of the Christian church,
thereby providing salvation
for all peoples, Gentiles and Jews.

Verily, verily, I say unto thee, Except a man be born again, he cannot see the kingdom of God.
JOHN 3:3

To be born again means
to accept Jesus as the Son of God
and to ask Him to forgive your sins.
Only after that can you start living all over
again, with the Holy Spirit—
Jesus' Spirit—residing inside you.

. . .I say unto you,
He that believeth on me
hath everlasting life.
I am that bread of life.

JOHN 6:47, 48

In your patience possess ye your souls.

LUKE 21:19

. . .Except a man be born of water and of the Spirit, he cannot enter into the kingdom of God. That which is born of the flesh is flesh; and that which is born of the Spirit is spirit. Marvel not that I said unto thee, Ye must be born again.

JOHN 3:5-7

If thou knowest the gift of God, and who it is that saith to thee, Give me to drink; thou wouldest have asked of him, and he would have given thee living water.   JOHN 4:10

*A Samaritan woman
encountered Jesus at a well and,
knowing He was a Jew,
was amazed that
He would ask her,
an enemy of the Jews,
for a drink of water.
But Jesus wanted to give this woman—
and wants to give all who come to Him—
the "water" of eternal life.*

Whosoever drinketh of this water shall thirst again: but whosoever drinketh of the water that I shall give him shall never thirst; but the water that I shall give him shall be in him a well of water springing up into everlasting life.   JOHN 4:13, 14

Verily, verily, I say unto you, He that heareth my word, and believeth on him that sent me, hath everlasting life, and shall not come into condemnation; but is passed from death unto life.

JOHN 5:24

My sheep hear my voice, and I know them, and they follow me: and I give unto them eternal life; and they shall never perish, neither shall any man pluck them out of my hand. My Father, which gave them me, is greater than all; and no man is able to pluck them out of my Father's hand.

JOHN 10:27-29

Labour not for the meat which perisheth, but for that meat which endureth unto everlasting life, which the Son of man shall give unto you: for him hath God the Father sealed.   JOHN 6:27

Say not ye, There are yet four months, and then cometh harvest? behold, I say unto you, Lift up your eyes, and look on the fields; for they are white already to harvest. And he that reapeth receiveth wages, and gathereth fruit unto life eternal: that both he that soweth and he that reapeth may rejoice together. JOHN 4:35, 36

*Those who share
their faith with others
will spend eternity with Jesus.*

And this is the will of him that sent me, that every one which seeth the Son, and believeth on him, may have everlasting life: and I will raise him up at the last day. JOHN 6:40

*The "last day" refers to
Jesus' Second Coming,
a day no one knows,
when Jesus will raise up
those who have
already died and
those still alive
who believed in Him.*

I am the living bread which came down from heaven: if any man eat of this bread, he shall live for ever: and the bread that I will give is my flesh, which I will give for the life of the world.

JOHN 6:51

I am the resurrection and the life: he that believeth in me, though he were dead, yet shall he live: and whosoever liveth and believeth in me shall never die. Believest thou this?

JOHN 11:25, 26

He that loveth his life shall lose it; and he that hateth his life in this world shall keep it unto life eternal. JOHN 12:25

To love your own life means
to become so absorbed with yourself
that you forget what is really important—
your love for God, and consequently,
your desire to do God's will.

Whither I go, thou canst not follow me now; but thou shalt follow me afterwards. JOHN 13:36

In my Father's house are many mansions: if it were not so, I would have told you. I go to prepare a place for you. And if I go and prepare a place for you, I will come again, and receive you unto myself; that where I am, there ye may be also.   JOHN 14:2, 3

. . .Thou hast given him [Jesus] power over all flesh, that he should give eternal life to as many as thou hast given him. And this is life eternal, that they might know thee the only true God, and Jesus Christ, whom thou hast sent.

JOHN 17:2, 3

Father, I will that they also, whom thou hast given me, be with me where I am; that they may behold my glory, which thou hast given me: for thou lovedst me before the foundation of the world.   JOHN 17:24

Yet a little while, and the world seeth me no more; but ye see me: because I live, ye shall live also. At that day ye shall know that I am in my Father, and ye in me, and I in you.   JOHN 14:19, 20

A woman when she is in travail hath sorrow, because her hour is come: but as soon as she is delivered of the child, she remembereth no more the anguish, for joy that a man is born into the world. And ye now therefore have sorrow: but I will see you again, and your heart shall rejoice, and your joy no man taketh from you.

JOHN 16:21, 22

WHY ARE JESUS' WORDS SO IMPORTANT?

*To grow in the Christian faith,
you need to spend time reading
the Bible, the source of all
wisdom and understanding.
There is no other way!
All of Jesus' words are contained in the Bible,
as well as hundreds of prophecies
that He alone fulfilled.*

. . .Man shall not live by bread alone, but by every word that proceedeth out of the mouth of God.   MATTHEW 4:4

Think not that I am come to destroy the law, or the prophets: I am not come to destroy, but to fulfil. For verily I say unto you, Till heaven and earth pass, one jot or one tittle shall in no wise pass from the law, till all be fulfilled.   MATTHEW 5:17, 18

Therefore whosoever heareth these sayings of mine, and doeth them, I will liken him unto a wise man, which built his house upon a rock: and the rain descended, and the floods came, and the winds blew, and beat upon that house; and it fell not: for it was founded upon a rock. And every one that heareth these sayings of mine, and doeth them not, shall be likened unto a foolish man, which built his house upon the sand: and the rain descended, and the floods came, and the winds blew, and beat upon that house; and it fell: and great was the fall of it.   MATTHEW 7:24-27

For this is he, of whom it is written, behold, I send my messenger before thy face, which shall prepare thy way before thee. For all the prophets and the law prophesied until John [the Baptist].   MATTHEW 11:10, 13

Ye do err, not knowing the scriptures, nor the power of God. . .have ye not read that which was spoken unto you by God, saying, I am the God of Abraham, and the God of Isaac, and the God of Jacob? God is not the God of the dead, but of the living.   MATTHEW 22:29, 31, 32

Because it is given unto you to know the mysteries of the kingdom of heaven, but to them it is not given. Therefore speak I to them in parables: because they seeing see not; and hearing they hear not, neither do they understand. And in them is fulfilled the prophecy of Esaias [Isaiah], which saith, By hearing ye shall hear, and ye shall not understand; and seeing ye shall see, and shall not perceive. For this people's heart is waxed gross, and their ears are dull of hearing, and their eyes they have closed; lest at any time they should see with their eyes and hear with their ears, and should understand with their heart, and should be converted, and I should heal them. But blessed are your eyes, for they see: and your ears, for they hear. MATTHEW 13:11, 13-16

Thinkest thou that I cannot now pray to my Father, and he shall presently give me more than twelve legions of angels? But how then shall the scriptures be fulfilled, that thus it must be? Are ye come out as against a thief with swords and staves for to take me? I sat daily with you teaching in the temple, and ye laid no hold on me. But all this was done, that the scriptures of the prophets might be fulfilled. MATTHEW 26:53–56

Heaven and earth shall pass away, but my words shall not pass away.

MATTHEW 24:35

A sower went out to sow his seed: and as he sowed, some fell by the way side; and it was trodden down, and the fowls of the air devoured it. And some fell upon a rock; and as soon as it was sprung up, it withered away, because it lacked moisture. And some fell among thorns; and the thorns sprang up with it, and choked it. And other fell on good ground, and sprang up, and bare fruit an hundredfold.

. . .Now the parable is this: The seed is the word of God. Those by the way side are they that hear; then cometh the devil, and taketh away the word out of their hearts, lest they should believe and be saved. They on the rock are they, which when they hear, receive the word with joy; and these have no root, which for a while believe, and in time of temptation fall away. And that which fell among thorns are they, which, when they have heard, go forth, and are choked with cares and riches and pleasures of this life, and bring no fruit to perfection. But that on the good ground are they, which in an honest and good heart, having heard the word, keep it, and bring forth fruit with patience.   LUKE 8:5-8; 11-15

The time is fulfilled, and the kingdom of God is at hand: repent ye, and believe the gospel.

MARK 1:15

My mother and my brethren are these which hear the word of God, and do it. LUKE 8:21

. . .Blessed are they that hear the word of God, and keep it. LUKE 11:28

The law and the prophets were until John [the Baptist]: since that time the kingdom of God is preached, and every man presseth into it. And it is easier for heaven and earth to pass, than one tittle of the law to fail.

LUKE 16:16, 17

These are the words which I spake unto you, while I was yet with you, that all things must be fulfilled, which were written in the law of Moses, and in the prophets, and in the psalms, concerning me. LUKE 24:44

For I have not spoken of myself;
but the Father which sent me,
he gave me a commandment,
what I should say,
and what I should speak.
And I know that his commandment is
life everlasting:
whatsoever I speak therefore,
even as the Father said unto me,
so I speak.

JOHN 12:49, 50

Thus it is written, and thus it behoved Christ to suffer, and to rise from the dead the third day: and that repentance and remission of sins should be preached in his name among all nations, beginning at Jerusalem. And ye are witnesses of these things.   LUKE 24:46-48

Search the scriptures; for in them ye think ye have eternal life: and they are they which testify of me.   JOHN 5:39

For had ye believed Moses, ye would have believed me: for he wrote of me. But if ye believe not his writings, how shall ye believe my words?
JOHN 5:46, 47

It is the spirit that quickeneth; the flesh profiteth nothing: the words that I speak unto you, they are spirit, and they are life.   JOHN 6:63

If ye continue in my word, then are ye my disciples indeed; and ye shall know the truth, and the truth shall make you free.   JOHN 8:31, 32

I and my Father are one.   JOHN 10:30

> *Jesus and God are one;*
> *thus, every word that Jesus spoke*
> *is perfect and true.*

Now ye are clean through the word which I have spoken unto you.   JOHN 15:3

If ye abide in me, and my words abide in you, ye shall ask what ye will, and it shall be done unto you.   JOHN 15:7

Sanctify them through thy truth: thy word is truth.   JOHN 17:17

What Is Worship?

Meeting with
other believers to
praise God and thank Him
for His unfathomable kindness
and blessings is another way to
grow in the Christian faith.
When you keep your eyes on Jesus,
selfish desires become less important
and God's will for your life
comes into sharper focus.
When you keep your eyes on Jesus,
you become part of the kingdom
of God on earth.

Get thee hence, Satan: for it is written, Thou shalt worship the Lord thy God, and him only shalt thou serve.   MATTHEW 4:10

Blessed art thou, Simon Bar-jona: for flesh and blood hath not revealed it unto thee, but my Father which is in heaven. And I say also unto thee, That thou art Peter, and upon this rock I will build my church; and the gates of hell shall not prevail against it.   MATTHEW 16:17, 18

Jesus is not promising
to build His church on Peter
but on Himself. As Jesus' disciple,
Peter would be instrumental
in starting Jesus' church.

For where two or three are gathered together in my name, there am I in the midst of them.
                                        MATTHEW 18:20

. . .It is written, My house shall be called the house of prayer; but ye have made it a den of thieves.   MATTHEW 21:13

For he is not a God of the dead, but of the living: for all live unto him.   LUKE 20:38

But the hour cometh, and now is, when the true worshippers shall worship the Father in spirit and in truth: for the Father seeketh such to worship him. God is a Spirit: and they that worship him must worship him in spirit and in truth.

JOHN 4:23, 24

Unto what is the kingdom of God like? . . .It is like a grain of mustard seed, which a man took, and cast into his garden; and it grew, and waxed a great tree; and the fowls of the air lodged in the branches of it. LUKE 13:18, 19

Whereunto shall I liken the kingdom of God? It is like leaven, which a woman took and hid in three measures of meal, till the whole was leavened.

LUKE 13:20, 21

The kingdom of God cometh not with observation: Neither shall they say, Lo here! or, lo there! for, behold, the kingdom of God is within you.

LUKE 17:20, 21

HOW SHOULD
I PRAY?

Talking to God—
spending time in prayer—
is easier when you
consider Him the perfect,
most understanding Father,
perhaps the father
you never had or knew.
Jesus as Son had
the most intimate knowledge of
His Father and
His words hold the key to
one of the greatest blessings
of the Christian life.

And when thou prayest, thou shalt not be as
the hypocrites are: for they love to pray standing in
the synagogues and in the corners of the streets,
that they may be seen of men. Verily I say unto
you, they have their reward.   MATTHEW 6:5

But thou, when thou prayest, enter into thy closet, and when thou hast shut thy door, pray to thy Father which is in secret; and thy Father which seeth in secret shall reward thee openly.   MATTHEW 6:6

But when ye pray, use not vain repetitions, as the heathen do: for they think that they shall be heard for their much speaking. Be not ye therefore like unto them: for your Father knoweth what things ye have need of, before ye ask him.
MATTHEW 6:7, 8

. . .Therefore pray ye: Our Father which art in heaven, Hallowed be thy name. Thy kingdom come. Thy will be done in earth, as it is in heaven. Give us this day our daily bread. And forgive us our debts, as we forgive our debtors. And lead us not into temptation, but deliver us from evil: For thine is the kingdom, and the power, and the glory, for ever. Amen.   MATTHEW 6:9-13

If ye then, being evil, know how to give good gifts unto your children, how much more shall your Father which is in heaven give good things to them that ask him?   MATTHEW 7:11

. . .I say unto you, That if two of you shall agree on earth as touching any thing that they shall ask, it shall be done for them of my Father which is in heaven. For where two or three are gathered together in my name, there am I in the midst of them.   MATTHEW 18:19, 20

And whatsoever ye shall ask in my name, that will I do, that the Father may be glorified in the Son. If ye shall ask any thing in my name, I will do it.   JOHN 14:13, 14

. . .Verily, verily, I say unto you, Whatsoever ye shall ask the Father in my name, he will give it you. Hitherto have ye asked nothing in my name: ask, and ye shall receive, that your joy may be full.   JOHN 16:23, 24

If ye abide in me,
and my words abide in you,
ye shall ask what ye will,
and it shall be done unto you.

JOHN 15:7

———◆◇◆———

How Can I
Ask Jesus To
Forgive Me?

(when I can't forgive others)

*Begin by
learning to love,
as Jesus loved,
and all things are possible.
Jesus knows your needs and
He will give you
strength to forgive—
and forget—
and then love
as never before.*

———◆———

But love ye your enemies, and do good. . .hoping
for nothing again; and your reward shall be great,
and ye shall be the children of the Highest: for he
is kind unto the unthankful and to the evil.

LUKE 6:35

Wherefore I say unto thee, Her sins, which are many, are forgiven; for she loved much: but to whom little is forgiven, the same loveth little.

LUKE 7:47

. . .Love your enemies, do good to them which hate you, bless them that curse you, and pray for them which despitefully use you. And unto him that smiteth thee on the one cheek offer also the other; and him that taketh away thy cloke forbid not to take thy coat also. . . .For if ye love them which love you, what thank have ye? . . .And if ye do good to them which do good to you, what thank have ye?

LUKE 6:27-29, 32, 33

Can a blind man lead a blind man? Will they not both fall into a pit?. . .Why do you look at the speck of sawdust in your brother's eye and pay not attention to the plank in your own eye? How can you say to your brother, "Brother, let me take the speck out of your eye," when you yourself fail to see the plank in your own eye? You hypocrite, first take the plank out of your eye, and then you will see clearly to remove the speck from your brother's eye.

LUKE 6:39-42 NIV

Greater love hath
no man than this,
that a man lay down
his life for his friends.
Ye are my friends,
if ye do whatsoever
I command you.

JOHN 15:13, 14

He that is without sin among you, let him first cast a stone. . . .   JOHN 8:7

Judge not according to the appearance, but judge righteous judgment.   JOHN 7:24

Ye have heard that it was said by them of old time, Thou shalt not kill; and whosoever shall kill shall be in danger of the judgment: But I say unto you, that whosoever is angry with his brother without a cause shall be in danger of the judgment. . .   MATTHEW 5:21, 22

For if ye forgive men their trespasses, your heavenly Father will also forgive you: But if ye forgive not men their trespasses, neither will your Father forgive your trespasses.   MATTHEW 6:14, 15

I say not unto thee, Until seven times: but until seventy times seven.   MATTHEW 18:22

In answer to Peter's question,
"Lord, how oft shall my brother sin against me,
and I forgive him? till seven times?"

. . .Thou shalt love the Lord thy God with all thy heart, and with all thy soul, and with all thy mind. This is the first and great commandment. And the second is like unto it, Thou shalt love thy neighbour as thyself. On these two commandments hang all the law and the prophets.   MATTHEW 22:37-40

A new commandment I give unto you, That ye love one another; as I have loved you, that ye also love one another. By this shall all men know that ye are my disciples, if ye have love one to another.
JOHN 13:34, 35

As the Father hath loved me, so have I loved you: continue ye in my love.   JOHN 15:9

These things I command you, that ye love one another.   JOHN 15:17

WHAT IS MERCY?

God the Father is a perfect,
just God who delights
in showing mercy
to those He loves.
When you ask His forgiveness,
His mercy is immediate and abundant.
Jesus' mercy is simply an extension of
the overwhelming love
He has for all His followers.

. . .He [the Father] maketh his sun to rise on the evil and on the good, and sendeth rain on the just and on the unjust.   MATTHEW 5:45

Judge not, that ye be not judged. For with what judgment ye judge, ye shall be judged: and with what measure ye mete, it shall be measured to you again.   MATTHEW 7:1, 2

. . .They that be whole need not a physician, but they that are sick. But go ye and learn what that meaneth, I will have mercy, and not sacrifice: for I am not come to call the righteous, but sinners to repentance.   MATTHEW 9:12, 13

The time is fulfilled, and the kingdom of God is at hand: repent ye, and believe the gospel.
                                        MARK 1:15

Unto you it is given to know the mystery of the kingdom of God: but unto them that are without, all these things are done in parables: That seeing they may see, and not perceive; and hearing they may hear, and not understand; lest at any time they should be converted, and their sins should be forgiven them.
                                        MARK 4:11, 12

. . .It is said, Thou shalt not tempt the Lord thy God.   LUKE 4:12

Be ye therefore merciful, as your Father also is merciful.   LUKE 6:36

. . .Hath no man
condemned thee? . . .
Neither do I condemn thee:
go, and sin no more.

JOHN 8:10, 11

———◆———

. . .Will not God bring about justice for his chosen ones, who cry out to him day and night? Will he keep putting them off? I tell you, he will see that they get justice, and quickly. However, when the Son of Man comes, will he find faith on the earth?　　　　　　LUKE 18:7, 8 NIV

"When the Son of Man comes. . ."
refers to Jesus' Second Coming,
an occurrence that will follow a time
of persecution for Christians.
Jesus will come again
to raise up His believers—
"justice" will be served—
both alive and dead.

For the Father judgeth no man, but hath committed all judgment unto the Son: That all men should honour the Son, even as they honour the Father. He that honoureth not the Son honoureth not the Father which hath sent him. Verily, verily, I say unto you, He that heareth my word, and believeth on him that sent me, hath everlasting life, and shall not come into condemnation; but is passed from death unto life.　　　JOHN 5:22-24

Father, forgive them; for they know not what they
do.   LUKE 23:34

I can of mine own self do nothing: as I hear, I
judge: and my judgment is just; because I seek
not mine own will, but the will of the Father
which hath sent me.

                                       JOHN 5:30

. . .For judgment I am come into this world, that
they which see not might see; and that they which
see might be made blind.   JOHN 9:39

*Those who refuse to believe in Jesus
are those who are then "made blind."*

And if any man hear my words, and believe not,
I judge him not: for I came not to judge the world,
but to save the world. He that rejecteth me, and
receiveth not my words, hath one that judgeth
him: the word that I have spoken, the same shall
judge him in the last day.   JOHN 12:47, 48

And I seek not mine own glory:
there is one that
seeketh and judgeth.
Verily, verily, I say unto you,
If a man keep my saying,
he shall never see death.

JOHN 8:50, 51

————◆————

Can Jesus Carry All My Burdens?

There is no burden
too great for Jesus,
no problem that He
hasn't encountered,
no situation too complex
for Him to understand.
He is above all things,
yet He is also the lowly servant,
One beaten and cursed,
One who gave His life
for His friend—you.

Come unto me, all ye that labour and are heavy laden, and I will give you rest. Take my yoke upon you, and learn of me; for I am meek and lowly in heart: and ye shall find rest unto your souls. For my yoke is easy, and my burden is light. MATTHEW 11:28-30

Blessed are they that mourn: for they shall be comforted. Blessed are the meek: for they shall inherit the earth.   MATTHEW 5:4, 5

. . .Take no thought for your life, what ye shall eat, or what ye shall drink; nor yet for your body, what ye shall put on. Is not the life more than meat, and the body than raiment? Behold the fowls of the air: for they sow not, neither do thy reap, nor gather into barns; yet your heavenly Father feedeth them. Are ye not much better than they?   MATTHEW 6:25, 26

Consider the lilies of the field, how they grow; they toil not, neither do they spin; and yet I say unto you, that even Solomon in all his glory was not arrayed like one of these. Wherefore, if God so clothe the grass of the field, which to day is, and to morrow is cast into the oven, shall he not much more clothe you, O ye of little faith?   MATTHEW 6:28-30

Take therefore no thought for the morrow: for the morrow shall take thought for the things of itself. Sufficient unto the day is the evil thereof.
                              MATTHEW 6:34

Therefore take no thought, saying, What shall we eat? or, What shall we drink? or, Wherewithal shall we be clothed? . . .for your heavenly Father knoweth that ye have need of all these things. But seek ye first the kingdom of God, and his righteousness; and all these things shall be added unto you.   MATTHEW 6:31-33

Be of good cheer; it is I; be not afraid.
                                                          MARK 6:50

Why are ye fearful, O ye of little faith?
                                                    MATTHEW 8:26

And fear not them which kill the body, but are not able to kill the soul: but rather fear him which is able to destroy both soul and body in hell.
                                                    MATTHEW 10:28

Are not two sparrows sold for a farthing? and one of them shall not fall on the ground without your Father. But the very hairs of your head are all numbered. Fear ye not therefore, ye are of more value than many sparrows.   MATTHEW 10:29-31

Blessed are
the poor in spirit:
for theirs is
the kingdom of heaven.

MATTHEW 5:3

Be not afraid, only believe.   MARK 5:36

Blessed be ye poor: for yours is the kingdom of God. Blessed are ye that hunger now: for ye shall be filled. Blessed are ye that weep now: for ye shall laugh. Blessed are ye, when men shall hate you, and when they shall separate you from their company, and shall reproach you, and cast out your name as evil, for the Son of man's sake. Rejoice ye in that day, and leap for joy: for behold, your reward is great in heaven: for in the like manner did their fathers unto the prophets.   LUKE 6:20-23

Daughter, be of good comfort: thy faith hath made thee whole; go in peace.   LUKE 8:48

> *Believing in Jesus*
> *guarantees our*
> *spiritual health—*
> *we can overcome*
> *the obstacles*
> *of poor health*
> *if we possess peace*
> *in our inner being.*

Fear not, little flock; for it is your Father's good pleasure to give you the kingdom.

LUKE 12:32

Let not your heart be troubled: ye believe in God, believe also in me. In my Father's house are many mansions: if it were not so, I would have told you. I go to prepare a place for you. And if I go and prepare a place for you, I will come again, and receive you unto myself: that where I am, there ye may be also. JOHN 14:1-3

. . .If a man have an hundred sheep, and one of them be gone astray, doth he not leave the ninety and nine, and goeth into the mountains, and seeketh that which is gone astray? And if so be that he find it, verily I say unto you, he rejoiceth more of that sheep, than of the ninety and nine which went not astray. Even so it is not the will of your Father which is in heaven, that one of these little ones should perish.

MATTHEW 18:12-14

Peace be unto you. JOHN 20:19

And now I am
no more in the world,
but these are in the world,
and I come to thee.
Holy Father, keep through
thine own name those
whom thou hast given me,
that they may be one,
as we are.

JOHN 17:11

Peace I leave with you, my peace I give unto you: not as the world giveth, give I unto you. Let not your heart be troubled, neither let it be afraid.

JOHN 14:27

Who Is
The Holy Spirit?

When you ask Jesus to
come into your heart,
the Holy Spirit—Jesus' Spirit—
comes to reside within you.
As you get to know
Jesus better through
His Word, prayer times, and worship,
you will recognize the voice
of the Holy Spirit,
guiding you to be as Jesus would want,
righteous, courageous, and humble.

And I will pray the Father, and he shall give you another Comforter, that he may abide with you for ever; even the Spirit of truth; whom the world cannot receive, because it seeth him not, neither knoweth him: but ye know him; for he dwelleth with you, and shall be in you.   JOHN 14:16, 17

But the Comforter, which is the Holy Ghost [Spirit], whom the Father will send in my name, he shall teach you all things, and bring all things to your remembrance, whatsoever I have said unto you.   JOHN 14:26

. . .It is expedient for you that I go away: for if I go not away, the Comforter will not come unto you; but if I depart, I will send him unto you. And when he is come, he will reprove the world of sin, and of righteousness, and of judgment: Of sin, because they believe not on me; of righteousness, because I go to my Father, and ye see me no more; of judgment, because the prince of this world [Satan] is judged.

JOHN 16:7-11

. . .When he, the Spirit of truth, is come, he will guide you into all truth: for he shall not speak of himself; but whatsoever he shall hear, that shall he speak: and he will shew you things to come. He shall glorify me: for he shall receive of mine, and shall shew it unto you.

JOHN 16:13, 14

. . .Wait for the promise of the Father, which. . .ye have heard of me. For John [the Baptist] truly baptized with water; but ye shall be baptized with the Holy Ghost. . . .   ACTS 1:4, 5

And when they bring you unto the synagogues, and unto magistrates, and powers, take ye no thought how or what thing ye shall answer, or what ye shall say: For the Holy Ghost shall teach you in the same hour what ye ought to say.
                    LUKE 12:11, 12

But ye shall receive power, after that the Holy Ghost is come upon you: and ye shall be witnesses unto me, both in Jerusalem, and in all Judaea, and in Samaria, and unto the uttermost part of the earth.   ACTS 1:8

But when the Comforter is come,
whom I will send unto you
from the Father,
even the Spirit of truth,
which proceedeth from the Father,
he shall testify of me:
And ye also shall bear witness,
because ye have been with me
from the beginning.

JOHN 15:26, 27

———◆◈◆———

WHO IS SATAN?

Satan, or Lucifer,
the angel thrown out of heaven
(*see* Revelation 12:7-12),
is the embodiment of
evil or sin on earth.
Until that day in the future
when Jesus banishes Satan
from the world forever
(*see* Isaiah 14:12-17;
Revelation 20:10),
this prince of darkness
remains the relentless purveyor
of all temptation,
corrupter of thoughts and actions,
and stalker of Christians.
Only a strong faith in Jesus
will keep you from succumbing
to Satan's ploys.

Beware of false prophets, which come to you in sheep's clothing, but inwardly they are ravening wolves. Ye shall know them by their fruits. Do men gather grapes of thorns, or figs of thistles? Even so every good tree bringeth forth good fruit; but a corrupt tree bringeth forth evil fruit.

MATTHEW 7:15-17

When an evil spirit comes out of a man, it goes through arid places seeking rest and does not find it. Then it says, "I will return to the house I left." When it arrives, it finds the house unoccupied, swept clean and put in order. Then it goes and takes with it seven other spirits more wicked than itself, and they go in and live there. And the final condition of that man is worse than the first. That is how it will be with this wicked generation.

MATTHEW 12:43-45 NIV

The person who has rid himself
of the evil spirit has not found Jesus,
but merely done this of his own volition.
Men and women are powerless
to save themselves.

Get thee behind me, Satan: thou art an offence unto me: for thou savourest not the things that be of God, but those that be of men. . . .For what is a man profited, if he shall gain the whole world, and lose his own soul? or what shall a man give in exchange for his soul?

MATTHEW 16:23, 26

Put up again thy sword into his place; for all they that take the sword shall perish with the sword.

MATTHEW 26:52

Satan is
the instigator of violence,
beginning a downward spiral
that leads only to death.

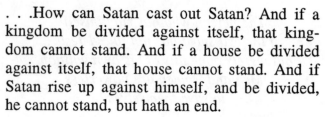

. . .How can Satan cast out Satan? And if a kingdom be divided against itself, that kingdom cannot stand. And if a house be divided against itself, that house cannot stand. And if Satan rise up against himself, and be divided, he cannot stand, but hath an end.

MARK 3:23-26

Watch ye and pray,
lest ye enter into temptation.
The spirit truly is ready,
but the flesh is weak.

MARK 14:38

. . .All manner of sin and blasphemy shall be forgiven unto men; but the blasphemy against the Holy Ghost shall not be forgiven unto men . . . whosoever speaketh against the Holy Ghost, it shall not be forgiven him, neither in this world, neither in the world to come.

MATTHEW 12:31, 32

To attribute
the miracles of Jesus—
performed in
the name of
the Holy Spirit—
to Satan is
the one and only
unforgivable sin.

He that is not with me is against me: and he that gathereth not with me scattereth.   LUKE 11:23

Why sleep ye? rise and pray, lest ye enter into temptation.   LUKE 22:46

The world cannot hate you; but me it hateth, because I testify of it, that the works thereof are evil. JOHN 7:7

. . .Whosoever committeth sin is the servant of sin. And the servant abideth not in the house for ever: but the Son abideth ever. If the Son therefore shall make you free, ye shall be free indeed. JOHN 8:36

Ye are of your father the devil, and the lusts of your father ye will do. He was a murderer from the beginning, and abode not in the truth, because there is no truth in him. When he speaketh a lie, he speaketh of his own: for he is a liar, and the father of it. And because I tell you the truth, ye believe me not. JOHN 8:44, 45

. . .Are there not twelve hours in the day? If any man walk in the day, he stumbleth not, because he seeth the light of this world. But if a man walk in the night, he stumbleth, because there is no light in him. JOHN 11:9, 10

. . .Yet a little while is the light with you. Walk while ye have the light, lest darkness come upon you: for he that walketh in darkness knoweth not whither he goeth. While ye have light, believe in the light, that ye may be the children of light.

JOHN 12:35, 36

Hereafter I will not talk much with you: for the prince of this world cometh, and hath nothing in me. But that the world may know that I love the Father; and as the Father gave me commandment, even so I do. . . .   JOHN 14:30, 31

What Does It Mean, Then, To Follow Jesus?

*To be a disciple
of Jesus is
the greatest privilege
ever bestowed,
yet the life of a Christian is
not without pain.*

Follow me, and I will make you fishers of men.

MATTHEW 4:19

Blessed are the pure in heart; for they shall see God. Blessed are the peacemakers: for they shall be called the children of God. Blessed are they which are persecuted for righteousness' sake: for theirs is the kingdom of heaven.

MATTHEW 5:9, 10

Blessed are ye, when men shall revile you, and persecute you, and shall say all manner of evil against you falsely, for my sake. Rejoice, and be exceeding glad: for great is your reward in heaven: for so persecuted they the prophets which were before you.   MATTHEW 5:11, 12

Ye are the salt of the earth: but if the salt have lost his savour, wherewith shall it be salted? it is thenceforth good for nothing, but to be cast out, and to be trodden under foot of men.

MATTHEW 5:13

Ye are the light of the world. A city that is set on an hill cannot be hid. Neither do men light a candle and put it under a bushel, but on a candlestick; and it giveth light unto all that are in the house. Let your light so shine before men, that they may see your good works, and glorify your Father which is in heaven.

MATTHEW 5:14-16

Follow me; and let the dead bury their dead.

MATTHEW 8:22

Enter ye in at the strait gate: for wide is the gate, and broad is the way, that leadeth to destruction, and many there be which go in thereat: Because strait is the gate, and narrow is the way, which leadeth unto life, and few there be that find it.

MATTHEW 7:13, 14

No man putteth a piece of new cloth unto an old garment, for that which is put in to fill it up taketh from the garment, and the rent is made worse. Neither do men put new wine into old bottles: else the bottles break, and the wine runneth out, and the bottles perish: but they put new wine into new bottles, and both are preserved.

MATTHEW 9:16, 17

When a person believes that
Jesus is the Son of God,
he becomes a different person from before.
Jesus, therefore, is the piece of new cloth,
the new wine, that is only accommodated
in a new garment or bottle.
One cannot remain the same
with Jesus directing one's life.

Blessed are they
which do hunger and
thirst after righteousness:
for they shall be filled.

MATTHEW 5:6

The disciple is not above his master, nor the servant above his lord. It is enough for the disciple that he be as his master, and the servant as his lord. MATTHEW 10:24, 25

What I tell you in darkness, that speak ye in light: and what ye hear in the ear, that preach ye upon the housetops. MATTHEW 10:27

Whosoever therefore shall confess me before men, him will I confess also before my Father which is in heaven. But whosoever shall deny me before men, him will I also deny before my Father which is in heaven.

MATTHEW 10:32, 33

He that loveth father or mother more than me is not worthy of me; and he that loveth son or daughter more than me is not worthy of me. And he that taketh not his cross, and followeth after me, is not worthy of me. He that findeth his life shall lose it: and he that loseth his life for my sake shall find it.

MATTHEW 10:37-39

. . .Who is my mother? and who are my brethren?
. . .Behold my mother and my brethren! For
whosoever shall do the will of my Father which
is in heaven, the same is my brother, and sister,
and mother.   MATTHEW 12:48-50

. . .It is given unto you to know the mysteries of the
kingdom of heaven. . . .For whosoever hath, to him
shall be given, and he shall have more abundance:
but whosoever hath not, from him shall be taken
away even that he hath.   MATTHEW 13:11, 12

. . .If ye have faith as a grain of mustard seed,
ye shall say unto this mountain, Remove hence to
yonder place; and it shall remove; and nothing
shall be impossible unto you.   MATTHEW 17:20

. . .Except ye be converted, and become as little
children, ye shall not enter into the kingdom of
heaven. Whosoever therefore shall humble himself as this little child, the same is greatest in the
kingdom of heaven. And whoso shall receive one
such little child in my name receiveth me.
                                        MATTHEW 18:3-5

. . .Whosoever will be great among you, let him be your minister; and whosoever will be chief among you, let him be your servant: Even as the Son of man came not to be ministered unto, but to minister, and to give his life a ransom for many. MATTHEW 20:26-28

For many are called, but few are chosen.
MATTHEW 22:14

But he that is greatest among you shall be your servant. And whosoever shall exalt himself shall be abased; and he that shall humble himself shall be exalted. MATTHEW 23:11, 12

. . .If thou canst believe, all things are possible to him that believeth. MARK 9:23

No man, when he hath lighted a candle, covereth it with a vessel, or putteth it under a bed; but setteth it on a candlestick, that they which enter in may see the light. LUKE 8:16

Return to thine own house, and shew how great
things God hath done unto thee.   LUKE 8:39

Blessed are the eyes which see the things that ye
see: For I tell you, that many prophets and kings
have desired to see those things which ye see, and
have not seen them; and to hear those things which
ye hear, and have not heard them.

LUKE 10:23, 24

No servant can serve two masters: for either he
will hate the one, and love the other; or else he will
hold to the one, and despise the other. Ye cannot
serve God and mammon [money].   LUKE 16:13

But he that doeth truth cometh to the light, that
his deeds may be made manifest, that they are
wrought in God.   JOHN 3:21

Thus the saying "One sows and another reaps" is
true. I sent you to reap what you have not worked
for. Others have done the hard work, and you
have reaped the benefits of their labor.

JOHN 4:37, 38 NIV

. . .Every plant,
which my heavenly Father
hath not planted,
shall be rooted up. . .
And if the blind
lead the blind,
both shall fall
into the ditch.

MATTHEW 15:13, 14

———————◆———————

Wilt thou be made whole? JOHN 5:6

All that the Father giveth me shall come to me; and him that cometh to me I will in no wise cast out. JOHN 6:37

. . .Therefore said I unto you, that no man can come unto me, except it were given unto him of my Father. JOHN 6:65

He that speaketh of himself seeketh his own glory: but he that seeketh his glory that sent him, the same is true, and no unrighteousness is in him. JOHN 7:18

. . .If any man thirst, let him come unto me, and drink. He that believeth on me, as the scripture hath said, out of his belly shall flow rivers of living water. JOHN 7:37, 38

I said therefore unto you, that ye shall die in your sins: for if ye believe not that I am he, ye shall die in your sins. JOHN 8:24

. . .If ye continue in my word, then are ye my disciples indeed; and ye shall know the truth, and the truth shall make you free.

JOHN 8:31, 32

If any man serve me, let him follow me; and where I am there shall also my servant be: if any man serve me, him will my Father honour.

JOHN 12:26

. . .He that believeth on me, believeth not on me, but on him that sent me. And he that seeth me seeth him that sent me.   JOHN 12:44, 45

If I wash thee not, thou hast no part with me.

JOHN 13:8

. . .He that believeth on me, the works that I do shall he do also; and greater works than these shall he do; because I go unto my Father.

JOHN 14:12

. . .I am the light of the world:
he that followeth me
shall not walk in darkness,
but shall have
the light of life.

JOHN 8:12

———◆❖◆———

Abide in me, and I in you. As the branch cannot bear fruit of itself, except it abide in the vine; no more can ye, except ye abide in me. . . Herein is my Father glorified, that ye bear much fruit; so shall ye be my disciples.

JOHN 15:4, 8

Henceforth I call you not servants; for the servant knoweth not what his lord doeth: but I have called you friends; for all things that I have heard of my Father I have made known unto you. JOHN 15:15

Ye have not chosen me, but I have chosen you, and ordained you, that ye should go and bring forth fruit, and that your fruit should remain: that whatsoever ye shall ask of the Father in my name, he may give it you.

JOHN 15:16

If the world hate you, ye know that it hated me before it hated you. JOHN 15:18

If ye were of the world, the world would love his own: but because ye are not of the world, but I have chosen you out of the world, therefore the world hateth you. . . .If they have persecuted me, they will also persecute you; if they have kept my saying, they will keep yours also. But all these things will they do unto you for my name's sake, because they know not him that sent me.   JOHN 15:19-21

They shall put you out of the synagogues: yea, the time cometh, that whosoever killeth you will think that he doeth God service. And these things will they do unto you, because they have not known the Father, nor me.   JOHN 16:2, 3

As thou [God the Father] hast sent me into the world, even so have I also sent them into the world. And for their sakes I sanctify myself, that they also might be sanctified through the truth.
          JOHN 17:18, 19

. . .Thomas, because thou hast seen me, thou hast believed: blessed are they that have not seen, and yet have believed.   JOHN 20:29

DID JESUS
ADDRESS THE
CONCERNS
OF TODAY?

*As the Son of God,
Jesus knew that His words
would be read by
candlelight and
halogen lamps,
and memorized
in upper rooms
and Sunday school classes.
And because human nature
has not changed
over the centuries—
we are still prone
to make the same mistakes—
the truth of Jesus' words
is untarnished.*

———◆———

Adultery, Lust

Ye have heard that it was said by them of old time, Thou shalt not commit adultery: But I say unto you, that whosoever looketh on a woman to lust after her hath committed adultery with her already in his heart.   Matthew 5:27, 28

. . .Whosoever shall put away [divorce] his wife, and marry another, committeth adultery against her. And if a woman shall put away [divorce] her husband, and be married to another, she committeth adultery.   Mark 10:11, 12

Benevolence
(the gift of giving)

And whosoever shall compel thee to go a mile, go with him twain. Give to him that asketh thee, and from him that would borrow of thee turn not thou away.   Matthew 5:41, 42

For I was an hungred, and ye gave me meat: I was thirsty, and ye gave me drink: I was a stranger, and ye took me in: Naked, and ye clothed me: I was sick, and ye visited me: I was in prison, and ye came unto me. . . . Verily I say unto you, Inasmuch as ye have done it unto one of the least of these my brethren, ye have done it unto me.

MATTHEW 25:36, 36, 40

So when you give to the needy, do not announce it with trumpets, as the hypocrites do in the synagogues and on the streets, to be honored by men. I tell you the truth, they have received their reward in full. But when you give to the needy, do not let your left hand know what your right hand is doing, so that your giving may be in secret. Then your Father, who sees what is done in secret, will reward you. MATTHEW 6:2-4 NIV

He that receiveth a prophet in the name of a prophet shall receive a prophet's reward; and he that receiveth a righteous man in the name of a righteous man shall receive a righteous man's reward. And whosoever shall give to drink unto one of these little ones a cup of cold water only in the name of a disciple, verily I say unto you, he shall in no wise lose his reward. MATTHEW 10:41, 42

Verily I say unto you, That this poor widow hath cast more in, than all they which have cast into the treasury: For all they did cast in of their abundance; but she of her want did cast in all that she had, even all her living.   MARK 12:43, 44

Give to every man that asketh of thee; and of him that taketh away thy goods ask them not again. And as ye would that men should do to you, do ye also to them likewise.   LUKE 6:30, 31

But when thou makest a feast, call the poor, the maimed, the lame, the blind: And thou shalt be blessed; for they cannot recompense thee: for thou shalt be recompensed at the resurrection of the just.
LUKE 14:13, 14

CHILDREN

Take heed that ye despise not one of these little ones; for I say unto you, that in heaven their angels do always behold the face of my Father which is in heaven.   MATTHEW 15:10

And whoso shall receive one such little child in my name receiveth me. But whoso shall offend one of these little ones which believe in me, it were better for him that a millstone were hanged about his neck, and that he were drowned in the depth of the sea.

MATTHEW 18:5, 6

. . .Suffer little children, and forbid them not, to come unto me: for of such is the kingdom of heaven.　　　　　　　　　MATTHEW 19:14

DIVORCE

It hath been said, Whosoever shall put away [divorce] his wife, let him give her a writing of divorcement: But I say unto you, That whosoever shall put away his wife, saving for the cause of fornication, causeth her to commit adultery: and whosoever shall marry her that is divorced committeth adultery.

MATTHEW 5:31, 32

. . .Moses because of the hardness of your hearts suffered you to put away your wives: but from the beginning it was not so.　　　MATTHEW 19:8

GOSSIP, PROFANITY

But I say unto you, Swear not at all; neither by heaven; for it is God's throne: Nor by the earth; for it is his footstool: neither by Jerusalem; for it is the city of the great King. Neither shalt thou swear by thy head, because thou canst not make one hair white or black. But let your communication be, Yea, yea; Nay, nay: for whatsoever is more than these cometh of evil.

MATTHEW 5:34-37

. . .How can ye, being evil, speak good things? for out of the abundance of the heart the mouth speaketh. . . .But I say unto you, That every idle word that men shall speak, they shall give account thereof in the day of judgment. For by thy words thou shalt be justified, and by thy words thou shalt be condemned.　　　MATTHEW 12:34, 36, 37

But those things which
proceed out of the mouth
come forth from the heart;
and they defile the man.
For out of the heart
proceed evil thoughts,
murders, adulteries, fornications,
thefts, false witness, blasphemies;
these are the things
which defile a man. . . .

MATTHEW 15:18-20

Not that which goeth into the mouth defileth a man; but that which cometh out of the mouth, this defileth a man.   MATTHEW 15:11

LEGAL ADVICE

Agree with thine adversary quickly, whiles thou art in the way with him; lest at any time the adversary deliver thee to the judge, and the judge deliver thee to the officer, and thou be cast into prison.   MATTHEW 5:25

Ye have heard that it hath been said, An eye for an eye, and a tooth for a tooth: But I say unto you, that ye resist not evil: but whosoever shall smite thee on thy right cheek, turn to him the other also. And if any man will sue thee at the law, and take away thy coat, let him have thy cloke also. And whosoever shall compel thee to go a mile, go with him twain.
                    MATTHEW 5:38-41

Moreover if thy brother shall trespass against thee, go and tell him his fault between thee and him alone: if he shall hear thee, thou hast gained thy brother. But if he will not hear thee, then take with thee one or two more, that in the mouth of two or three witnesses every word may be established. And if he shall neglect to hear them, tell it unto the church: but if he neglect to hear the church, let him be unto thee as an heathen and a publican.

MATTHEW 18:15-17

. . .Render therefore unto Caesar the things which are Caesar's; and unto God the things that are God's.   MATTHEW 22:21

. . .In the world ye shall have tribulation: but be of good cheer; I have overcome the world.

JOHN 16:33

Marriage

. . .Have ye not read, that he [God] which made them at the beginning made them male and female, and said, For this cause shall a man leave father and mother, and shall cleave to his wife, and they twain shall be one flesh? Wherefore they are no more twain, but one flesh. What therefore God hath joined together, let not man put asunder.   Matthew 19:4-6

Wealth, Worldly Success

No man can serve two masters: for either he will hate the one, and love the other; or else he will hold to the one, and despise the other. Ye cannot serve God and mammon [money].

Matthew 6:24

Lay not up for yourselves treasures upon earth, where moth and rust doth corrupt, and where thieves break through and steal: But lay up for yourselves treasures in heaven, where neither moth nor rust doth corrupt, and where thieves do not break through nor steal: For where your treasure is, there will your heart be also.　　MATTHEW 6:19-21

Therefore take no thought, saying What shall we eat? or What shall we drink? or, Wherewithal shall we be clothed? . . .for your heavenly Father knoweth that ye have need of all these things. But seek ye first the kingdom of God, and his righteousness; and all these things shall be added unto you.　　　　　MATTHEW 6:31-33

If thou wilt be perfect, go and sell that thou hast, and give to the poor, and thou shalt have treasure in heaven: and come and follow me.

MATTHEW 19:21

*Jesus wants
to be the treasure
of your life,
not worldly possessions.*

But woe unto you that are rich! for ye have received your consolation. Woe unto you that are full! for ye shall hunger. Woe unto you that laugh now! for ye shall mourn and weep. Woe unto you, when all men shall speak well of you! for so did their fathers to the false prophets.

LUKE 6:24-26

Take heed, and beware of covetousness: for a man's life consisteth not in the abundance of the things which he possesseth.   LUKE 12:15

He that is faithful in that which is least is faithful also in much: and he that is unjust in the least is unjust also in much. If therefore ye have not been faithful in the unrighteous mammon, who will commit to your trust the true riches?

LUKE 16:10, 11

. . .Ye are they which justify yourselves before men; but God knoweth your hearts: for that which is highly esteemed among men is abomination in the sight of God.   LUKE 16:15

. . .Many that are first
shall be last;
and the last
shall be first.

Matthew 19:30

How hardly shall they that have riches enter into the kingdom of God! For it is easier for a camel to go through a needle's eye, than for a rich man to enter into the kingdom of God.

LUKE 18:24, 25

How can ye believe, which receive honour one of another, and seek not the honour that cometh from God only? JOHN 5:44

What Did
Jesus Say
To Teachers,
To Missionaries?

*There will always
be a need for
teachers and missionaries,
those who will not be deterred
by inevitable obstacles,
those who feel called by God
to share Jesus' words.*

Give not that which is holy unto the dogs, neither cast ye your pearls before swine, lest they trample them under their feet, and turn again and rend you.   MATTHEW 7:6

*Teach only what
your students have
the capacity to learn.*

The harvest truly is plenteous,
but the labourers are few;
pray ye therefore the Lord
of the harvest,
that he will send forth
labourers into his harvest.

MATTHEW 9:37, 38

But go rather to the lost sheep of the house of Israel. And as ye go, preach, saying, The kingdom of heaven is at hand.   MATTHEW 10:6, 7

Behold, I send you forth as sheep in the midst of wolves: be ye therefore wise as serpents, and harmless as doves.   MATTHEW 10:16

Whosoever therefore shall confess me before men, him will I confess also before my Father which is in heaven.   MATTHEW 10:32

. . .All power is given unto me in heaven and in earth. Go ye therefore, and teach all nations, baptizing them in the name of the Father, and of the Son, and of the Holy Ghost: Teaching them to observe all things whatsoever I have commanded you: and, lo, I am with you alway, even unto the end of the world.

MATTHEW 28:18-20

Peace be unto you: as my Father hath sent me, even so send I you.   JOHN 20:21

. . .Take nothing for your journey. . .and whatsoever house ye enter into, there abide, and thence depart. And whosoever will not receive you, when ye go out of that city, shake off the very dust from your feet for a testimony against them.   LUKE 9:3-5

. . .No man, having put his hand to the plough, and looking back, is fit for the kingdom of God.
                                                 LUKE 9:62

PART III:

His Return

———————

WHAT ARE SOME SIGNS THAT JESUS' SECOND COMING IS NEAR?

*Many of the signs
Jesus described have been
or are being fulfilled
in the world today.
While Jesus delays His coming,
there's still time to make sure your
family will be joining you in heaven.
There's still time,
as Isaiah says, to be
"a highway for our God."*

When it is evening, ye say, It will be fair weather: for the sky is red. And in the morning, It will be foul weather to day: for the sky is red and lowring. O ye hypocrites, ye can discern the face of the sky; but can ye not discern the signs of the times? MATTHEW 16:2, 3

And the brother shall deliver up the brother to death, and the father the child: and the children shall rise up against their parents, and cause them to be put to death. And ye [all believers in Jesus] shall be hated of all men for my name's sake: but he that endureth to the end shall be saved. But when they persecute you in this city, flee ye into another: for verily I say unto you, Ye shall not have gone over the cities of Israel, till the Son of man be come.

MATTHEW 10:21-23

. . .Take heed that no man deceive you. For many shall come in my name, saying, I am Christ; and shall deceive many. And ye shall hear of wars and rumours of wars: see that ye be not troubled: for all these things must come to pass, but the end is not yet. for nation shall rise against nation, and kingdom against kingdom: and there shall be famines, and pestilences, and earthquakes, in divers places. All these are the beginning of sorrows.

MATTHEW 24:4-8

And this gospel of the kingdom
shall be preached
in all the world for
a witness unto all nations;
and then shall the end come.

MATTHEW 24:14

The days will come, when ye shall desire to see one of the days of the Son of man, and ye shall not see it. And they shall say to you, See here; or, see there: go not after them, nor follow them.

LUKE 17:22, 23

And then shall many be offended, and shall betray one another, and shall hate one another. And many false prophets shall rise, and shall deceive many. And because iniquity shall abound, the love of many shall wax cold. But he that shall endure unto the end, the same shall be saved.

MATTHEW 24:10-13

And as it was in the days of Noe [Noah], so shall it be also in the days of the Son of man. They did eat, they drank, they married wives, they were given in marriage, until the day that Noe entered into the ark, and the flood came, and destroyed them all. Likewise also as it was in the days of Lot; they did eat, they drank, they bought, they sold, they planted, they builded; but the same day that Lot went out of Sodom it rained fire and brimstone from heaven, and destroyed them all. Even thus shall it be in the day when the Son of man is revealed.

LUKE 17:26-30

And there shall be signs in the sun, and in the moon, and in the stars; and upon the earth distress of nations, with perplexity; the sea and the waves roaring. Men's hearts failing them for fear, and for looking after those things which are coming on the earth: for the powers of heaven shall be shaken. . . .And when these things begin to come to pass, then look up, and lift up your heads; for your redemption draweth nigh.

LUKE 21:25, 26, 28

O Jerusalem, Jerusalem, thou that killest the prophets, and stonest them which are sent unto thee, how often would I have gathered thy children together, even as a hen gathereth her chickens under her wings, and ye would not! Behold, your house is left unto you desolate. For I say unto you, Ye shall not see me henceforth, till ye shall say, Blessed is he that cometh in the name of the Lord. MATTHEW 23:37-39

How Will Jesus Appear When He Comes Again?

From many accounts
throughout the Scriptures
we know Jesus will appear
to His believers in the clouds.
The only question
that remains is when,
and that is not for us to know.
Keep looking up!

. . .Ye shall see the Son of man sitting on the right hand of power, and coming in the clouds of heaven.   MARK 14:62

For whosoever shall be ashamed of me and of my words, of him shall the Son of man be ashamed, when he shall come in his own glory, and in his Father's, and of the holy angels.   LUKE 9:26

Be ye therefore ready also: for the Son of man cometh at an hour when ye think not.   LUKE 12:40

I tell you, in that night [that Jesus returns] there shall be two men in one bed; the one shall be taken, and the other shall be left. Two women shall be grinding together; the one shall be taken, and the other left. Two men shall be in the field; the one shall be taken, and the other left.

LUKE 17:34-36

And then shall they see the Son of man coming in a cloud with power and great glory.

LUKE 21:27

Verily, verily, I say unto you, The hour is coming, and now is, when the dead shall hear the voice of the Son of God: and they that hear shall live. . . .Marvel not at this: for the hour is coming, in the which all that are in the graves shall hear his voice, and shall come forth; they that have done good, unto the resurrection of life; and they that have done evil, unto the resurrection of damnation.   JOHN 5:25, 29

But of that day and that hour knoweth no man, no, not the angels which are in heaven, neither the Son, but the Father. Take ye heed, watch and pray: for ye know not when the time is. For the Son of man is as a man taking a far journey, who left his house, and gave authority to his servants, and to every man his work, and commanded the porter to watch. Watch ye therefore: for ye know not when the master of the house cometh, at even, or at midnight, or at the cockcrowing, or in the morning: Lest coming suddenly he find you sleeping. And what I say unto you I say unto all, Watch.   MARK 13:32-37

ARE YOU
READY TO
MEET JESUS?

*Someday all believers
will have such an opportunity,
a moment that defies
human imagination.*

When the Son of man shall come in his glory, and all the holy angels with him, then shall he sit upon the throne of his glory: And before him shall be gathered all nations: and he shall separate them one from another, as a shepherd divideth his sheep from the goats: And he shall set the sheep on his right hand, but the goats on the left. Then shall the King say unto them on his right hand, Come, ye blessed of my Father, inherit the kingdom prepared for you from the foundation of the world.   MATTHEW 25:31-34

And take heed to yourselves, lest at any time your hearts be overcharged with surfeiting, and drunkenness, and cares of this life, and so that day come upon you unawares. For as a snare shall it come on all them that dwell on the face of the whole earth. Watch ye therefore, and pray always, that ye may be accounted worthy to escape all these things that shall come to pass, and to stand before the Son of man.

LUKE 21:34-36

By "all these things
that shall come to pass"
Jesus is referring to
a time of great tribulation,
following His appearance
in the clouds,
when all those
who have not accepted Jesus
will be subjected to
horrible occurrences.
At the end of the tribulation
Jesus will then come
back to earth to establish
His permanent kingdom,
"the New Jerusalem."

When ye therefore shall see the abomination of desolation, spoken of by Daniel the prophet, stand in the holy place, (whoso readeth, let him understand:) Then let them which be in Judaea flee into the mountains: Let him which is on the housetop not come down to take any thing out of his house; neither let him which is in the field return back to take his clothes. And woe unto them that are with child, and to them that give suck in those days! But pray ye that your flight be not in the winter, neither on the sabbath day: For then shall be great tribulation, such as was not since the beginning of the world to this time, no, nor ever shall be. And except those days should be shortened, there should no flesh be saved: but for the elect's sake those days shall be shortened.

MATTHEW 24:16-22

This is a further description
of the time of great tribulation.
The "abomination of desolation"
refers to the antichrist,
or Satan in human form,
who will assume world power
during this time.

Immediately after the tribulation of those days shall the sun be darkened, and the moon shall not give her light, and the stars shall fall from heaven, and the powers of the heavens shall be shaken: And then shall appear the sign of the Son of man in heaven: and then shall all the tribes of the earth mourn, and they shall see the Son of man coming in the clouds of heaven with power and great glory. And he shall send his angels with a great sound of a trumpet, and they shall gather together his elect from the four winds, from one end of heaven to the other.

MATTHEW 24:29-31

*Following the tribulation
Jesus will make His
triumphant return to
the New Jerusalem,
having gathered together
those believers who rose
earlier to meet Him in the clouds
and those new believers
on earth who accepted Jesus
during the tribulation.*

As therefore the tares are gathered and burned in the fire; so shall it be in the end of this world. The Son of man shall send forth his angels, and they shall gather out of his kingdom all things that offend, and them which do iniquity; and shall cast them into a furnace of fire: there shall be wailing and gnashing of teeth. Then shall the righteous shine forth as the sun in the kingdom of their Father. . . .

Matthew 13:40-43

Before Jesus establishes
His New Jerusalem,
all who have refused to
believe in Him
will be sent to hell,
to a place
of eternal torment.
The "righteous,"
those who believe,
will live forever
in the light with Jesus.

For as the lightning,
that lighteneth out of
the one part under heaven,
shineth unto the
other part under heaven;
so shall also
the Son of man
be in his day.

LUKE 17:24

APPENDIX

Who Is Jesus?
(Reflections by those who met Him)

And the Word was made flesh, and dwelt among us, (and we beheld his glory, the glory as of the only begotten of the Father,) full of grace and truth.

—John the disciple, JOHN 1:14

Throughout his gospel,
John, who was perhaps
Jesus' most beloved friend on earth,
describes the Son of God with
compassion and authority.
To know Jesus as the Word—
Logos, *in the Greek—*
is to believe Him to embody
all the treasures of divine wisdom.

And, behold, thou shalt conceive in thy womb, and bring forth a son, and shalt call his name JESUS. He shall be great, and shall be called the Son of the Highest: and the Lord God shall give unto him the throne of his father David: And he shall reign over the house of Jacob for ever; and of his kingdom there shall be no end.

—Angel Gabriel to Mary, Jesus' earthly mother, LUKE 1:31-33

Blessed art thou among women, and blessed is the fruit of thy womb. And whence is this to me, that the mother of my Lord should come to me? For, lo, as soon as the voice of thy salutation sounded in mine ears, the babe leaped in my womb for joy.

—Elizabeth, the mother of John the Baptist,
LUKE 1:42-44

Elizabeth, who was unaware
that her cousin Mary
would give birth to Jesus,
greeted her with these words,
having been filled with Holy Spirit.

———◆———

And she shall bring forth a son, and thou shalt call his name JESUS: for he shall save his people from their sins.

—Angel of the Lord to Joseph,
MATTHEW 1:21

For unto you is born this day in the city of David a Saviour, which is Christ the Lord. And this shall be a sign unto you; Ye shall find the babe wrapped in swaddling clothes, lying in a manger.

—Angel of the Lord to shepherds,
LUKE 2:11, 12

Lord, now lettest thou thy servant depart in peace, according to thy word: For mine eyes have seen thy salvation, which thou hast prepared before the face of all people; a light to lighten the Gentiles, and the glory of thy people Israel.

—Simeon, LUKE 2:29-32

God had revealed to Simeon,
a holy man, that he would not die
until he had seen the Christ.
When Joseph and Mary brought Jesus to
the temple shortly after His birth,
Simeon took the baby in his arms
and blessed Him,
and then praised God
for giving him that privilege.

———◆———

Where is he that is born King of the Jews? for we have seen his star in the east, and are come to worship him.

—Wise men to King Herod,
MATTHEW 2:2

This was he of whom I spake, He that cometh after me is preferred before me: for he was before me.

—John the Baptist, JOHN 1:15

**Behold the Lamb of God,
which taketh away
the sin of the world.**

John the Baptist
JOHN 1:29

———◆———

I baptize with water: but there standeth one among you, whom ye know not; He it is, who coming after me is preferred before me, whose shoe's latchet I am not worthy to unloose.

—John the Baptist,
JOHN 1:26, 27

I saw the Spirit descending from heaven like a dove, and it abode upon him. And I knew him not: but he that sent me to baptize with water, the same said unto me, Upon whom thou shalt see the Spirit descending, and remaining on him, the same is he which baptizeth with the Holy Ghost. And I saw, and bare record that this is the Son of God.

—John the Baptist,
JOHN 1:32-34

John the Baptist
baptized Jesus
and then witnessed the Spirit of God
coming down from heaven like
a dove to rest on Him.
Near the end of his ministry
John made the following powerful
declarations about Jesus.

Ye yourselves bear me witness, that I said, I am not the Christ, but that I am sent before him. . .He must increase, but I must decrease. He that cometh from above is above all: he that is of the earth is earthly, and speaketh of the earth: he that cometh from heaven is above all. And what he hath seen and heard, that he testifieth; and no man receiveth his testimony. He that hath received his testimony hath set to his seal that God is true. For he whom God hath sent speaketh the words of God: for God giveth not the Spirit by measure unto him. The Father loveth the Son, and hath given all things into his hand. He that believeth on the Son hath everlasting life: and he that believeth not the Son shall not see life; but the wrath of God abideth on him.

—John the Baptist, JOHN 3:28, 30-36

We have found the Messias [Messiah], which is, being interpreted, the Christ.

—Andrew the disciple, JOHN 1:41

We have found him, of whom Moses in the law, and the prophets, did write, Jesus of Nazareth, the son of Joseph.

—Philip the disciple, JOHN 1:45

Rabbi, thou art the Son of God; thou art the King of Israel.

> —Nathanael the disciple, JOHN 1:49

Rabbi, we know that thou art a teacher come from God: for no man can do these miracles that thou doest, except God be with him.

> —Nicodemus, JOHN 3:2

Lord, if thou wilt, thou canst make me clean.

> —Man with leprosy, MATTHEW 8:2

Behold, Lord, the half of my good I give to the poor; and if I have taken any thing from any man by false accusation, I restore him fourfold.

> —Zacchaeus, LUKE 19:8

Before encountering Jesus,
Zacchaeus was a less than
scrupulous tax collector,
a man in a reviled profession who
had made his situation even worse.
Convicted of his sin, and with his eyes on Jesus,
Zacchaeus now pledged to change his ways
and rectify his wrongdoing.

Lord,
I am not worthy that thou
shouldest come under my roof:
but speak the word only,
and my servant shall be healed.

Centurion
MATTHEW 8:8

———✦———

What manner of man is this, that even the winds and the sea obey him!

> —Jesus' disciples,
> MATTHEW 8:27

What have we to do with thee, Jesus, thou Son of God? art thou come hither to torment us before the time?

> —Demons that possessed two men,
> MATTHEW 8:2

> *Even Satan and his demons*
> *acknowledge Jesus*
> *as the Son of God.*

If I may but touch his garment, I shall be whole.
—Woman afflicted with bleeding disorder, who, upon touching Jesus' garment, was healed,
MATTHEW 9:21

It was never so seen in Israel.
—Crowd, upon witnessing Jesus' miracles,
MATTHEW 9:33

I know thee who thou art, the Holy One of God.
>—Man possessed of unclean spirit,
>MARK 1:24

Come, see a man, which told me all things that ever I did: is not this the Christ?
>—Samaritan woman Jesus met at a well,
>JOHN 4:29

Now we believe, not because of thy saying: for we have heard him ourselves, and know that this is indeed the Christ, the Saviour of the world.
>—Reaction of Samaritans after meeting Jesus,
>JOHN 4:42

Of a truth thou art the Son of God.
>—Reaction of disciples after Jesus
>calmed the storm at sea,
>MATTHEW 14:33

Thou art the Christ, the Son of the living God.
>—Peter the disciple,
>MATTHEW 16:16

A great prophet
is risen up among us. . .
God hath visited his people.

Crowd, upon witnessing Jesus raising the
widow of Nain's son from the dead
LUKE 7:16

Hosanna to the son of David.

> —Children in the synagogue,
> MATTHEW 21:15

From whence hath this man these things? and what wisdom is this which is given unto him, that even such mighty works are wrought by his hands? Is not this the carpenter, the son of Mary, the brother of James, and Joses, and of Juda, and Simon? and are not his sisters here with us?

> —Reaction of Nazarenes,
> MARK 6:2, 3

Lord, if thou hadst been here, my brother had not died. But I know, that even now, whatsoever thou wilt ask of God, God will give it thee. Yea, Lord: I believe that thou art the Christ, the Son of God, which should come into the world.

> —Martha, the sister of Lazarus,
> JOHN 11:21, 22, 27

After this Jesus approached the tomb
of Lazarus and displayed His
inestimable power as the Son of God
by bringing Lazarus, now dead four days,
back to life.

Now are we sure that thou knowest all things, and needest not that any man should ask thee: by this we believe that thou camest forth from God.

> —Jesus' disciples, upon hearing Jesus predict His death and resurrection,
>
> JOHN 16:30

Art thou the Christ? . . .Art thou then the Son of God? . . .What need we any further witness? for we ourselves have heard of his own mouth.

> —Members of the Sanhedrin before Jesus' crucifixion,
>
> LUKE 22: 67-71

Dost not thou fear God, seeing thou art in the same condemnation? And we indeed justly; for we receive the due reward of our deeds: but this man hath done nothing amiss. . . Jesus, Lord, remember me when thou comest into thy kingdom.

> —One of two criminals crucified with Jesus,
> Luke 23:40-42

Truly this was the Son of God.
　　—Centurion and others who witnessed Jesus'
crucifixion and the accompanying earthquake,
　　　　　　　　　　　　MATTHEW 27:54

Fear not ye: for I know that ye seek Jesus, which
was crucified. He is not here: for he is risen, as
he said. Come, see the place where the Lord lay.
　　　　　　　　　—Angel at Jesus' tomb,
　　　　　　　　　　　　MATTHEW 28: 5, 6

Did not our heart burn within us, while he talked
with us by the way, and while he opened to us the
scriptures?
　　　　　　　—Men on the road to Emmaus who
　　　　　　　　　walked with the risen Jesus,
　　　　　　　　　　　　LUKE 24:32

Lord, thou knowest all things; thou knowest that
I love thee.
　　　　　　　—Peter the disciple with the risen Jesus,
　　　　　　　　　　　　John 21:17

But these are written,
that ye might believe that
Jesus is the Christ,
the Son of God;
and that believing ye might
have life through his name.

John the disciple
JOHN 20:31

THE
BEATITUDES

Blessed are the poor in spirit: for theirs is the kingdom of heaven.

Blessed are they that mourn: for they shall be comforted.

Blessed are the meek: for they shall inherit the earth.

Blessed are they which do hunger and thirst after righteousness: for they shall be filled.

Blessed are the merciful: for they shall obtain mercy.

Blessed are the pure in heart: for they shall see God.

Blessed are the peacemakers: for they shall be called the children of God.

Blessed are they which are persecuted for righteousness' sake: for theirs is the kingdom of heaven.

Blessed are ye, when men shall revile you, and persecute you, and shall say all manner of evil against you falsely, for my sake.

MATTHEW 5:3-11

Rejoice, and be exceeding glad:
for great is your reward in heaven:
for so persecuted they the prophets
which were before you.

MATTHEW 5:12

———◆◈◆———

THE
LORD'S PRAYER

Our Father which art in heaven,
Hallowed be thy name.
Thy kingdom come.
Thy will be done in earth,
as it is in heaven.
Give us this day our daily bread.
And forgive us our debts,
as we forgive our debtors.
And lead us not into temptation,
but deliver us from evil:
For thine is the kingdom,
and the power, and
the glory, for ever.
Amen.

MATTHEW 6:9-13

PARABLE OF THE GOOD SAMARITAN

A certain man went down from Jerusalem to Jericho, and fell among thieves, which stripped him of his raiment, and wounded him, and departed, leaving him half dead.

And by chance there came down a certain priest that way: and when he saw him, he passed by on the other side.

And likewise a Levite, when he was at the place, came and looked on him, and passed by on the other side.

But a certain Samaritan, as he journeyed, came where he was: and when he saw him, he had compassion on him, and went to him, and bound up his wounds, pouring in oil and wine, and set him on his own beast, and brought him to an inn, and took care of him.

And on the morrow when he departed, he took out two pence, and gave them to the host, and said unto him, Take care of him; and whatsoever thou spendest more, when I come again, I will repay thee.

LUKE 10: 30-35

Which now of these three,
thinkest thou,
was neighbour unto him
that fell among the thieves? . . .
Go, and do thou likewise.

LUKE 10: 36–37

———◆———

PARABLE OF THE LOST SON

A certain man had two sons: And the younger of them said to his father, Father, give me the portion of goods that falleth to me. And he divided unto them his living.

And not many days after the younger son gathered all together, and took his journey into a far country, and there wasted his substance with riotous living.

And when he had spent all, there arose a mighty famine in that land; and he began to be in want.

And he went and joined himself to a citizen of that country; and he sent him into his fields to feed swine.

And he would fain have filled his belly with the husks that the swine did eat: and no man gave unto him.

And when he came to himself, he said, How many hired servants of my father's have bread enough and to spare, and I perish with hunger!

I will arise and go to my father, and will say unto him, Father, I have sinned against heaven, and before thee, and am no more worthy to be called thy son: make me as one of thy hired servants.

And he arose, and came to his father. But when he was yet a great way off, his father saw him, and had compassion, and ran, and fell on his neck, and kissed him.

And the son said unto him, Father, I have sinned against heaven, and in thy sight, and am no more worthy to be called thy son.

But the father said to his servants, Bring forth the best robe, and put it on him; and put a ring on his hand, and shoes on his feet.

And bring hither the fatted calf, and kill it; and let us eat, and be merry:

For this my son was dead, and is alive again; he was lost, and is found. And they began to be merry.

Now his elder son was in the field: and as he came and drew night to the house, he heard music and dancing.

And he called one of the servants, and asked what these things meant.

And he said unto him, Thy brother is come; and thy father hath killed the fatted calf, because he hath received him safe and sound.

And he was angry, and would not go in: therefore came his father out, and intreated him.

And he answering said to his father, Lo, these many years do I serve thee, neither transgressed I at any time thy commandment: and yet thou never gavest me a kid, that I might make merry with my friends:

But as soon as this thy son was come, which hath devoured thy living with harlots, thou hast killed for him the fatted calf.

And he said unto him, Son, thou art ever with me, and all that I have is thine.

LUKE 15:11-31

It was meet that
we should make merry,
and be glad:
for this thy brother was dead,
and is alive again;
and was lost,
and is found.

LUKE 15:32

Inspirational Library

Beautiful purse/pocket size editions of Christian classics bound in flexible leatherette. These books make thoughtful gifts for everyone on your list, including yourself!

The Bible Promise Book   Over 1000 promises from God's Word arranged by topic. What does God promise about matters like: Anger, Illness, Jealousy, Love, Money, Old Age, and Mercy? Find out in this book!
    Flexible Leatherette $3.97

Daily Light   One of the most popular daily devotionals with readings for both morning and evening.
    Flexible Leatherette $4.97

Wisdom from the Bible   Daily thoughts from Proverbs which communicate truths about ourselves and the world around us.
    Flexible Leatherette $4.97

My Daily Prayer Journal   Each page is dated and features a Scripture verse and ample room for you to record your thoughts, prayers, and praises. One page for each day of the year.
    Flexible Leatherette $4.97

Available wherever books are sold.
Or order from:

Barbour Publishing, Inc.
P.O. Box 719
Uhrichsville, OH 44683
http://www.barbourbooks.com

If you order by mail add $2.00 to your order for shipping.
Prices subject to change without notice.